Connect Online

www.connectonline.glencoe.com

Take-Home Activities

Gwen Solomon • Lynne Schrum

New York, New York   Columbus, Ohio   Chicago, Illinois   Peoria, Illinois   Woodland Hills, California

Glencoe/McGraw-Hill

A Division of The McGraw·Hill Companies

Copyright © 2003 by the McGraw-Hill Companies, Inc. All rights reserved. Permission is granted to reproduce the material contained herein on the condition that such materials be reproduced only for classroom use; be provided to students, teachers, and families without charge; and be used solely in conjunction with the *Connect Online: Web Learning Adventures* program. Any other reproduction, for sale or other use, is expressly prohibited.

Send all inquiries to:
Glencoe/McGraw-Hill
21600 Oxnard Street
Suite 500
Woodland Hills, CA 91367

ISBN: 0-07-824520-6 *Student Edition*
ISBN: 0-07-824521-4 *Teacher Manual and Key*
ISBN: 0-07-825154-0 *Take-Home Activities*

Printed in the United States of America.

1 2 3 4 5 6 7 8 9 10 071 05 04 03 02 01 00 99

Connect Online
Web Learning Adventures

Table of Contents

How-To Activities
- **Activity 1** **Mathematics** Build Bridges ... 1
- **Activity 2** **Art and Music** Fold Paper (Make Your Own Hummingbird) ... 3
- **Activity 3** **Science** Play With Water ... 5
- **Activity 4** **Home Economics** Build a Birdhouse ... 7
- **Activity 5** **Mathematics** Repeating Patterns ... 9
- **Activity 6** **Home Economics** Knit and Crochet ... 11
- **Activity 7** **Science** Plant a Garden ... 13

Interactive Activities
- **Activity 1** **Computer Science** Design a Robot ... 15
- **Activity 2** **Science** Dinosaur Days ... 17
- **Activity 3** **Social Studies** Exploring the Past ... 19
- **Activity 4** **Science** Extreme Weather—Hurricane Tracking ... 21
- **Activity 5** **Science** Life Underground ... 23
- **Activity 6** **Economics** Taking Stock ... 25
- **Activity 7** **Science** Seeing Is Believing ... 27
- **Activity 8** **Science** Roller Coaster Physics ... 29
- **Activity 9** **Mathematics** Oak Trees and Squirrels—Population Growth and Balance ... 31
- **Activity 10** **Science** Tiger Adventures ... 33

Exploration Activities
- **Activity 1** **Social Studies** Country of Beauty—Belize ... 35
- **Activity 2** **Science** Deserts—What Are They? ... 37
- **Activity 3** **Social Studies** A Person From History—Anne Frank ... 39
- **Activity 4** **Science** Who's a Rube? ... 41
- **Activity 5** **Science** Mars—the Red Planet ... 43
- **Activity 6** **Health and Fitness** Sports Alive! ... 45
- **Activity 7** **Health and Fitness** Pets To Love ... 47
- **Activity 8** **Economics** Get a Job! ... 49
- **Activity 9** **Social Studies** The United Nations ... 51
- **Activity 10** **Computer Science** Virtual Tours ... 53
- **Activity 11** **Science** Keeping Watch ... 55
- **Activity 12** **Art and Music** Take Note ... 57

About the Authors

Gwen Solomon is Director of TechLearning.com. Prior to this, she was Senior Analyst in the U.S. Department of Education's Office of Educational Technology. In the past, Gwen worked for the New York City Public Schools as Coordinator of Instructional Technology Planning and as founding Director of New York City's School of the Future. She was also a teacher and technology coordinator. Gwen is a past Chair of the Consortium for School Networking (CoSN).

Lynne Schrum is an Associate Professor in the Department of Instructional Technology at the University of Georgia. She received an M.A. in Elementary Education and Learning Disabilities from the University of Evansville, and in 1991, a Ph.D. in Curriculum and Instruction from the University of Oregon. Prior to her university work, she taught in elementary schools. Lynne is a past president of the International Society for Technology in Education (ISTE).

To the Parent and Teacher

Activities in this booklet are designed to educate and to stimulate students' interests. Although the Web sites used were carefully reviewed, they may be moved, removed, or altered after this book's publication. Therefore, a responsible adult should always preview Web sites to ensure that they still contain the activities described in the text. We encourage teachers, parents, and guardians to ask students what they are doing on the computer and to monitor students' behavior online.

The student edition of *Connect Online: Web Learning Adventures* contains information and activities on Internet safety and responsible online behavior. We suggest that parents and guardians ask their children what they know about these topics and discuss this information before they perform any activities at home. Since the Web sites noted in this booklet are all live sites, parents or guardians should supervise their children when they perform these activities at home.

To the Student

We chose the activities for this Take-Home Activity booklet to demonstrate that learning online is both fun and educational. Be sure to read guidelines carefully before performing an activity. If you have any questions or concerns, please check with your teacher or your parents or guardians. In fact, you might want to share these activities with your parents or guardians and even your brothers or sisters so that they can enjoy learning online too. If you follow these simple suggestions, you can all have a fun—and safe—learning experience at home.

Curriculum Connections Chart

Art and Music
Art
  Fold Paper (Make Your Own Hummingbird) 3
Music
  Take Note 57

Computer Science
Computer Science
  Virtual Tours 53
Robotics
  Design a Robot 15

Economics
Career Education
  Get a Job! 49
Economics
  Taking Stock 25

Health and Fitness
Health
  Pets to Love 47
Physical Fitness
  Sports Alive! 45

Home Economics
Home Economics
  Knit and Crochet 11
Industrial Arts
  Build a Birdhouse 7

Mathematics
Geometry
  Build Bridges 1
  Repeating Patterns 9
Probability/Modeling
  Oak Trees and Squirrels—Population Growth and Balance 31

Science
Archaeology
  Dinosaur Days 17
Astronomy
  Mars—the Red Planet 43
Chemistry
  Play With Water 5
Earth Science
  Deserts—What Are They? 37
Ecology
  Tiger Adventures 33
Geology
  Life Underground 23
Horticulture
  Plant a Garden 13
Meteorology
  Extreme Weather—Hurricane Tracking 21
Perception
  Seeing Is Believing 27
Physics
  Roller Coaster Physics 29
  Who's a Rube? 41
Zoology
  Keeping Watch 55

Social Studies
American History
  Exploring the Past 19
Current Events
  The United Nations 51
Geography
  Country of Beauty—Belize 35
History
  A Person From History—Anne Frank 39

Name _____ Date _____

How-To Activity
Subject Area: Mathematics

Build Bridges

Prepare
Have you ever wondered why igloos are dome-shaped and not cube-shaped? Have you ever been amazed at how a suspension bridge can hold the weight of hundreds of passing cars with little or no apparent support underneath it? Have you ever wondered how strong eggshells are? On a scale from 1 to 5, with 1 being very weak and 5 being very strong, how would you rate the eggs that are in your refrigerator now?

Perform
<http://www.spartechsoftware.com/reeko/Experiments/ExpEggShellArches.htm>
Try the experiment at Reeko's Mad Scientist Lab. This experiment demonstrates how arches are used in architecture not only to look good but also for structural purposes. You'll need four eggs, some tape, and several books for this experiment. After you follow the directions, you'll discover that arches—even those made of eggshells—are strong. The crown of an eggshell can support heavy books because the weight is distributed evenly along the structure of the egg. *Now that you have tried this experiment, why do you think arches are so strong?*

Related Web Site
Mobius Strip
<http://www.spartechsoftware.com/reeko/Experiments/ExpMobiusStrip.htm>
Learn a little more about geometry with this intriguing experiment. First, decide if you're sure you know inside from outside. Look at a glass of water. Well, that's pretty obvious. Look at a box—it's easy to tell the inside from the outside of a box also. But in this experiment, you may find that sometimes inside and outside are the same. *What is topology?*

Connect Online: Web Learning Adventures

Name _____ Date _____

How-To Activity
Subject Area: Art and Music

 **Fold Paper (Make Your Own Hummingbird)**

Prepare
What do you know about origami, the ancient Japanese art of folding paper into intricate shapes that represent animals and other objects? Have you ever tried to fold paper into a recognizable shape? For example, most kids like to make paper planes and fly them as best they can. Have you done this? If so, do you follow instructions or just fold the paper into a shape that looks like it can fly?

Perform
<http://www.paperfolding.com>
For this activity, you'll use the Web site called Eric's Origami Page. Watch the home page's graphic load, and then select the section "Learn to Fold." On this page you'll find interesting designs by a number of people. You can amaze your family and friends by creating these yourself. For example, select "Hummingbird" by Collin Weber. You'll find a page of diagrams with instructions you can follow onscreen or print out to do later. *Which project at this site would you like to try first? Why?*

Related Web Site
Origami Help for Beginners
<http://www.empnet.com/woodmansee/origuide.htm>
As you may have discovered, paper folding only looks simple. To do it correctly, you need skill and practice. For example, your folding lines should be creased properly, and all the edges should be lined up perfectly. Otherwise, the object you create may not look like what it is supposed to be. This site is a good place to start if you really want to develop your technique. *What is the best piece of advice you found at this Web site?*

Name _____   Date _____

How-To Activity
Subject Area: Science

Play With Water

Prepare
Current events in school are usually about things in the news and how they relate to history (and sometimes to you). But Bill Nye, the Science Guy, sees "current events" differently. He's looking at ocean currents. Water is often in the news. Whether water is part of a report on extreme weather, such as a hurricane or a flood, or whether water pollution or drought is the issue, water is very important in everyone's life.

Perform
<http://www.nyelabs.com/>
Go to the link for this activity and select "Home Demos." Then click "Planetary Science," "Earth Science," and "Current Event." With this experiment, you can study ocean currents by playing with water. You'll need a glass baking dish, a little salt, food coloring (blue, of course), and ice cubes. You'll mix salt and water, freeze and then melt it, and add an ice cube. What do you think will happen? Print out the instructions and try this experiment to find out. You'll learn that ocean currents are driven by the flow of heat and salt in the ocean. *Why is this experiment called a "current" event?*

Related Web Site
U.S. Geological Survey's (USGS) Water Science for Schools
<http://ga.water.usgs.gov/edu/index.html>
What is it about water that makes it water? This Web site examines the physical and chemical properties of water and shows why living things need it. You'll explore acid rain, why the ocean is salty, and how to measure water quality. You can even answer questions about how much water you use at home and compare your answers with those of students elsewhere.

After looking through the site, consider these questions: What do you think will be the biggest water problem of the next decade? How much water does a leaking faucet waste in a week? Do you know how many baths you could get from a rainstorm? This Web site also has a glossary. *Identify five new water words that you think you'll be able to use in school and find their definitions.*

Name _____ Date _____

How-To Activity
Subject Area: Home Economics

Build a Birdhouse

Prepare
Have you ever watched the birds in your neighborhood and wondered how to get a few of them to sing near your home? One way is to build a birdhouse and place it in an appropriate location. In this activity, you are going to print instructions for building a birdhouse. You'll also find out exactly what you need to attract possible tenants to your birdhouse.

Perform
<http://www.npwrc.usgs.gov/resource/tools/birdhous/birdhous.htm>
This site presents step-by-step directions for building a terrific birdhouse. You will need to make sure you have the right tools, equipment, and materials. Once you have built the birdhouse, you can continue with other construction activities. *Have you seen birdhouses in your neighborhood? What do you think is the most challenging part about building a birdhouse?*

Related Web Site
Birdhouse Plans
<http://www.choosefreedom.com/birdhouse.html>
This site lets you download directions for a traditional kind of birdhouse and shows you the way to build it. After you build one birdhouse, you can use your creativity to adapt the plans in unique ways. *Draw an original birdhouse. How would you go about constructing this birdhouse?*

Name _____ Date _____

How-To Activity
Subject Area: Mathematics

Activity 5: Repeating Patterns

Prepare
<http://library.thinkquest.org/16661/mosaics.html>
Visit this site and take a look at the design that appears under the link "Tilings of Regular Polygons." What can you see in this design? What shapes are prominent? What other shapes do you see? What pattern do you see? How easy do you think it is to create a design like this? Have you noticed how the design repeats?

The pattern you see and the others at this Web site are called tessellations. In a *tessellation,* the shapes must interlock and repeat to create a pattern. As you will see, tessellations are fascinating and complicated. This Web site will give you a good introduction to tessellations and to the mathematical theories behind them. Tessellations are beautiful and are used in many forms of art. You'll see quite a few examples of the work of Dutch artist M.C. Escher, whose designs are famous.

Perform
<http://library.thinkquest.org/16661>
High school students created the Totally Tessellated Web site located at the above URL so that you can learn about tessellations too. Go through this site to learn what they are and what math is involved. Start with the Essentials section and then read the background information. Next choose the Mosaics/Tilings section to learn about changing and creating tessellations. When you are sure that you understand what's involved, create your own. You could begin by adapting a tessellation that you see on the screen. In short, you can become totally tessellated too. *After you read about tessellations, find some mathematical terms associated with them. What does each term mean?*

Related Web Site
Coolmath Tessellations
<http://www.coolmath4kids.com/tesspag1.html>
This Coolmath site provides step-by-step information on creating tessellations and provides examples of how some types of tessellations look. *What do you think is the easiest way to create a tessellation?*

Name _____ Date _____

How-To Activity
Subject Area: Home Economics

Knit and Crochet

Prepare
Have you ever watched friends or relatives sew, knit, crochet, or needlepoint? If you learn a craft like this now, it will stay with you the rest of your life, and you will never regret having spent the time to learn it. Here is a way to get started!

Perform
<http://www.learntocrochet.com/>
Start with the basics—learn to knit or crochet. With just yarn and a few tools, you can create a blanket, a sweater, or a great scarf. This site will provide you with all the information you need to get started and to succeed. *What three things would you like to make, and what questions do you have before you get started?*

Related Web Site
Knit, Crochet, and More
<http://www.craftyarncouncil.com/>
This is the site of the Craft and Yarn Council. You can find out a lot of information about how to choose yarn, where to go for lessons, how to get started, and more. *Describe what you have learned and what you want to make first.*

Connect Online: Web Learning Adventures

Name _____ Date _____

How-To Activity
Subject Area: Science

 **Plant a Garden**

Prepare
Gardening is the number one outdoor hobby in America. You can get good exercise as well as grow beautiful flowers or tasty vegetables. Just being outside and seeing the results of your efforts is worth all the work. This activity will provide you with a wide range of information on how to get started with gardening.

Perform
<http://www.raw-connections.com/garden/>
The first steps in creating any kind of garden are planning and then planting. This link will take you to a site that gives you the chance to plant a garden, from start to finish. Be sure to read the directions before you start. Are you planning to grow flowers or vegetables? *What things will you need to consider before you get started?*

Related Web Site
Hawaii Tropical Botanical Garden
<http://www.htbg.com/>
You may have visions of a small garden on your windowsill, or you may be planning a large garden in the backyard. Regardless, take a few minutes to visit a very big garden—one of the botanical gardens of Hawaii. When you get to this site, scroll down and click "Take a Virtual Tour." This inspiration may help you decide what to put in your own garden. *Which section of the garden did you like the most? Why?*

Connect Online: Web Learning Adventures

Name _____   Date _____

Interactive Activity
Subject Area: Computer Science

Activity 1: Design a Robot

Prepare
Have you ever wished you had a robot who could do the chores your parents give you—like cleaning your room, walking the dog, or carrying out the trash? There are a million things we wish we could avoid doing or that we think robots could do better. Someday, we may be able to get robots to be our personal assistants. Meanwhile, at this Web site you'll learn how robots work today. You can also find out how robots are being used to do serious tasks for NASA.

Perform
<http://prime.jsc.nasa.gov/ROV/>
In this activity, you'll design a robot that can perform tasks in outer space. First read the information about robotics, find out about the mission goals, and learn facts about orbiting in space. Based on what you've learned, you'll build and program a virtual robot to accomplish a task for a NASA mission. You'll select parts that match functions such as propulsion, electric power, navigation, and inspection.

You'll have a choice of missions. One that involves the International Space Station (ISS) has the goals of navigating to various locations on the ISS and performing tasks. The second set of simulated environments is based on exploring Mars.

Once you've completed your robot, you'll program it and put it into a three-dimensional virtual environment. *Which mission did you select? Describe your robot, its task, and how well it performed.*

Related Web Site
Get a Grip on Robotics
<http://www.thetech.org/exhibits_events/online/robots/teaser/>
This online exhibit from the Tech Museum of Innovation will help you understand how robots work and help you predict their potential abilities for the future. Learn how robotic arms probe, grab, sense, lift, work, help, and move their way into our daily lives. Shake the robot's gripper to "Get a Grip on Robotics." *What are some tasks that you expect robots to do in the future?*

Connect Online: Web Learning Adventures

Name _____   Date _____

Interactive Activity
Subject Area: Science

Dinosaur Days

Prepare
What was it like to live in the time of the dinosaurs? What were these huge and mysterious creatures really like, and what kind of world did they live in? Books and movies present us with a world no one knows firsthand but almost everyone likes to imagine. In this activity, you can look at dinosaurs from the inside out—by moving dinosaur bones around to build your very own beast. Then you'll learn a great deal about dinosaurs.

Perform
<http://dsc.discovery.com/guides/dinosaur/dinosaur.html>
Go to the Web site listed below and select the link to "Interactive Game: Build a Beast!" Once in the game, use your cursor to drag bones from the dig to the dinosaur outline. You'll get a new clue with each bone so that eventually you can figure out what dinosaur you are creating. When it's complete, you can see your creation in several different views.

Other pages at the Dinosaur Guide let you check out dinosaur facts and fantasy. You can look at a dinosaur in motion to see how it behaved. You'll also learn about the latest finds and see special dinosaur sights, such as dinosaur babies and the largest dinosaur ever. If you're ready to hunt for your own dinosaurs, you'll learn how to locate your own fossils and check out some dinosaur adventures. For example, you can take a trip to "Valley of the T-REX" to see video clips and listen to audio clips of the scientist who is busy at work finding incredible artifacts. *What are some things that some people believe are true about dinosaurs that you now know the real truth about?*

Related Web Site
Dinorama
<http://www.nationalgeographic.com/dinorama/frame.html>
This National Geographic Web site has information about dinosaurs and different ways to learn about them. It includes timelines, animations, and

Connect Online: Web Learning Adventures   17

fun facts. For example, check out "Dinosaur Eggs," where you'll take an online egg hunt to see how researchers "hatch" fossilized dinosaur eggs to reveal the embryos inside. Go to the Dinorama "Dinosaur Eggs" page and then select "feature" from the "Learn More" box to enter the online egg hunt. *What are some things about dinosaurs that you would still like to learn?*

Name _____ Date _____

Interactive Activity
Subject Area: Social Studies

ACTIVITY 3 Exploring the Past

Prepare
Archaeologists dig through the remnants of ancient civilizations to learn about the lives and times of our ancestors. Historians study the everyday lives of people who lived in the more recent past by looking at clues—the objects and documents that people left behind that have somehow survived. What do you think such items can tell us about people's lives?

Perform
<http://americanhistory.si.edu/ve/index.htm>
One can only guess at the meaning of the mummies and pots and tools found in archaeological sites in faraway places. It's a little easier to understand what it was like in more recent times—for example, during the earlier years of the United States. In this activity, you'll discover what life was like for five families who lived in the same house in Ipswich, Massachusetts. Go to the Web site listed above from the National Museum of American History at the Smithsonian. Select "Within These Walls" to read about the lives of the families that lived in this house and to see some of the artifacts that remain from past times.

When you've finished checking out what life may have been like for the five families above, you can think about what historians in the next century could learn about you if they found your home (or your room!) exactly the way it is today. *What are some artifacts from your home that you think would be interesting for people to find 200 years from now?*

Related Web Site
Library of Congress
<http://memory.loc.gov/ammem/wpaposters/wpahome.html>
The Library of Congress has many artifacts that help us to understand more about the lives of people in various eras of American history. The "By the People, for the People: Posters from the WPA, 1936–1943" exhibition contains a collection of 900 boldly colored posters that were

produced as part of President Roosevelt's New Deal. These striking silkscreens, lithographs, and woodcuts were created to publicize health and safety programs; cultural programs, including art exhibitions and theatrical and musical performances; travel and tourism; educational programs; and community activities. *Which poster did you like the best?*

Name _____   Date _____

Interactive Activity
Subject Area: Science

 **Extreme Weather—Hurricane Tracking**

Prepare
Can you imagine your home's roof blowing off or trees in the park being uprooted? Can you picture a wind so fierce that if you try to walk toward it, you're blown backwards? If you were in a car or school bus, does it seem possible that you could be forced off the road because it flooded? These things happen during some seasons of the year in certain places in the United States. People have to worry about terrible weather that brings high winds and driving rain in the form of hurricanes. If you lived in an area that was prone to hurricanes, how would you know what to expect?

Perform
<http://www.riverdeep.net/earthpulse/data/earthpulse/earthpulsecenter.html>
In this activity, you'll play the role of a weather scientist. Go to Riverdeep's Earthpulse Center. Download Simplayer the first time you visit, and then you can go to the Hurricane Lab from the Control Room to find out what a hurricane is really like. First, you'll predict the path of hurricanes at the Forecasting Desk by tracking current or past storms. You'll take a virtual field trip to hurricane territory. By the time you've finished experimenting with this hurricane simulation, you'll be an expert—ready to talk to real weather scientists. *What would you do to prepare for a hurricane if one was approaching your town right now?*

Related Web Site

Hurricanes: The Greatest Storms on Earth
<http://hurricanes.noaa.gov/>
You'll find background information, a list of retired hurricane names, satellite imagery, tracking models, and more at this Web site from the National Oceanic and Atmospheric Administration (NOAA). The National Hurricane Center keeps an eye on tropical cyclones over the North Atlantic, the Caribbean Sea, the Gulf of Mexico, and the eastern North Pacific Ocean during hurricane season—roughly from June through November 30. *What does it mean that a hurricane name is retired?*

Interactive Activity
Subject Area: Science

Life Underground

Prepare

What kinds of trees and plants grow where you live? Do you know what they need to survive? For plants to grow, there must be the right combination of elements, such as soil, moisture, and sunlight. There's also more than the naked eye can see at work beneath the ground. Underground there's a complete environment made up of organisms that work together to help plants survive.

The major components underground are decomposers, plant-eaters, and predators. Decomposers eat the dead matter in the soil and turn it into nutrients for plants. Tiny decomposers or microbes such as bacteria and fungi change dying plant material into nutrients that plants need to grow. Plant-eaters nibble plants so that those plants become needed dead matter. If there are too many plant-eaters, however, they'll eat so many plants that nothing will be left to grow. Predators keep this plant-eater population in check. Predators eat plant-eating animals, including other predators. Together, these elements create a balanced environment.

Perform

<http://www.fieldmuseum.org/ua/>

In this activity, you'll create your own ecosystem in a virtual terrarium. Go to the Field Museum in Chicago's Underground Adventure Web site and select the virtual terrarium. You'll try to keep the environment in this terrarium balanced—and keep your plants alive—for as long as you can. You decide how many of each plant and organism to put into the terrarium. Then you will see how these organisms interact and will monitor what happens over time.

You can increase your odds of keeping the plants alive longer by mastering more information. You can learn about the world of soil from the other parts of the Field Museum's Underground Adventure. For example, you can take a virtual tour of a micro soil lab and try other scientific experiments alongside real scientists. You can even turn yourself into a

Connect Online: Web Learning Adventures

bug and explore the soil from the perspective of a smaller being. *Pretend that you're the bug that explored the soil at this Web site. How does the world look from a bug's point of view?*

Related Web Site

Microbe!
<http://www.microbe.org/>
At this site from the American Society for Microbiology, you can find out lots of information and have some fun too. First there are activities you can do with items that are probably already in your home. You can make a mess with dirt, paint, pond water, and other yucky stuff to find microbes. Next you'll join Sam Sleuth and help him perform detective work to find out about microbes. You'll discover what microbes are, where they live, why they're considered an "evolutionary success story," whether they're good or bad, and how they're used. *Are microbes good or bad?*

Name _____ Date _____

Interactive Activity
Subject Area: Economics

Taking Stock

Prepare

You've heard stories about Internet millionaires and people who made fortunes by buying stock in a company before the company became a hot property. Although everyone wants to become a millionaire, it's not easy to accumulate that kind of wealth. Over the last few decades, the stock market has been a good place to invest money. Even though you may have heard about lots of recent losses, there have also been gains for people who have held stocks for a long time. This is because, in the long run, gains often outweigh losses in the stock market.

Perform

<http://library.thinkquest.org/10326>

In this activity, not only will you learn how to invest in stocks, but you will also get some real practice in working with the stock market. InvestSmart, a ThinkQuest Web site, provides investment basics, investment lessons, a glossary of financial terms, and real-life examples of how three students got started in investing. You'll learn about investing in the stock market and mutual funds, and you'll see how the power of compounding can make you a millionaire even if you invest only $100 a month. After you have learned about stocks, bonds, mutual funds, and taxes, try the stock market simulation, where you can invest $100,000 of fantasy money. *Do you understand what happened to the economy in the last few years? What do you think happened to someone who invested $100,000 in 1998 if that person didn't sell the stocks in 2000?*

Related Web Site

Escape From Knab
<http://www.escapefromknab.com>

This simulation places you on the planet of Knab. You have to earn enough money to get back to Earth. Find out if you know enough about money and investing to earn your way back home! First you choose a job and complete a W-4 form so you can pay income tax. You'll decide how much money you want to take home each month and what it

Connect Online: Web Learning Adventures

means to withhold money for your taxes. You'll set up a budget and continue to manage your money as well as possible to reach the goal of earning $10,000 for your ticket home. *Did you get back home from Knab by July 4? How did you make most of the money you needed to buy your ticket?*

Name _____ Date _____

Interactive Activity
Subject Area: Science

Seeing Is Believing

Prepare

Optical illusions are fun to try, but have no illusions about them: optical illusions are based on real science. Illusions trick your eyes and brain into getting the wrong impression about an object you look at. No matter how long you look or how much you squint, you see the object inaccurately. Of course, knowing that you are seeing the object inaccurately doesn't change your perception of it. That's why such tricks of the eye are called optical illusions—they look different from the way they should look. Some optical illusions involve color shifts, others involve lines that appear to move, and some involve judging the sizes of objects. We'll see how well you see things.

Perform

<http://www.sandlotscience.com/>
It's all a matter of perspective. Visit the site called Sandlot Science. Select the "Moon Illusion" under "More Illusions" and then click the moon to start the interactive display. You'll move the moon around with your mouse and watch it grow. Can what you see be possible? Read the facts, and then be sure to check it out for real when it's dark outside.

Now try some of the other illusions posted at the Sandlot Science Web site under the "Illusions" head. If you like shapes, try Impossible Objects like "Crazy Crate" and "Endless Staircase." If you like twists, try Distortion Illusions like "Breathing Objects" and "Twisted Cord." If you like uncertainty, try Ambiguous Illusions like "Spinning Wheel" or "Rabbit Duck." *What was your favorite illusion?*

Related Web Site

Exploratorium
<http://www.exploratorium.edu/exhibits/f_exhibits.html>
The Exploratorium's Online Exhibits in the Learning Studio provide some fun optical illusions. You can stare at a dot to make it move, see a bird's shadow appear in a birdcage, watch a design shimmer, and more. You'll learn why you see these things the way you do. *Which optical illusion at this site is the most interesting? Why?*

Connect Online: Web Learning Adventures

Interactive Activity
Subject Area: Science

Roller Coaster Physics

Prepare
What's your favorite amusement park ride? Why do you like these parks and the kinds of rides you find there? Do you know what makes the rides work? This site will give you a new perspective into the scariest rides and will show you why you have fun at amusement parks.

For the most part, you visit an amusement park to have fun and to get a little bit scared. Some rides are more daring than others, and some people like the excitement. A lot of people scream—more from exhilaration than from fear. Have you ever thought about what makes a scary ride work? After all, you get on the highest and fastest rides believing that you'll wind up safe and sound when you get off. The answer to what makes the rides work is physics. Physics is the science that governs how amusement park rides operate.

Perform
<http://www.learner.org/exhibits/parkphysics/coaster>
In this activity, you will design your very own roller coaster. Even if you aren't an expert in physics or don't like to compute difficult mathematical formulas, this activity is for you. You'll decide a few things, like how high the first hill should be, what shape you want it to have, and how you get down. Then you'll decide on how high the second hill is and add a loop. When your roller coaster is ready to roll, you'll take it for a safety inspection first. *When does the roller coaster go the fastest?*

Related Web Site

Amuse Me: A Website on the Physics of Amusement Parks
<http://library.thinkquest.org/C005075F>
Have you ever wondered why a Ferris wheel doesn't fall over or why a roller coaster is able to climb such steep inclines? You can certainly ride any of these rides without ever considering the science on which they are based. This ThinkQuest site will help you understand the physical principles of different amusement park rides, particularly the great

thriller—the roller coaster. Many principles of physics are covered, including gravity, acceleration, drag, friction, and other laws of motion. *How many roller coasters have you ridden?*

Interactive Activity
Subject Area: Mathematics

Activity 9: Oak Trees and Squirrels—Population Growth and Balance

Prepare

Have you ever watched a tree over time or observed the behavior of squirrels? How do trees and squirrels influence each other, and how do scientists predict danger or overpopulation in a given environment? This site will give you a new perspective into the work that scientists do. You will use an actual computer model, implemented as a Java applet, to do hands-on control of an ecosystem.

The importance of both mathematical and computer models in the study of population growth are described and analyzed. This will give you a good understanding of the tools used by population ecologists. These ecologists research and uncover interesting facts about each population in order to understand the interaction between them. One of the main goals in recognizing the delicate balance between ecosystems and population growth is the development of a deeper understanding of nature and the environment.

Perform

<http://www.arcytech.org/java/population/>

In this activity, you will participate in a scientific adventure. First you will learn something about models and how a computer aids in understanding what is happening. Read the introduction and the letter to students at this site. You may want to show the letter to your parents and teachers too. Next, read about how to use the model, and select "Oak Trees" as a good place to start. Next, you may want to try the same activity with the item "Squirrels." *What did you learn about population and growth at this site?*

Related Web Site

Population Models
<http://www.syslab.ceu.hu/model_summaries/>
At this site you will explore the population dynamics models of various scientists. These are models and ideas of what might happen in the future with given populations. It is worthwhile to know how scientists estimate what will happen in the future. *Which model did you explore? What did you learn from this model?*

Name _____ Date _____

Interactive Activity
Subject Area: Science

ACTIVITY 10 — Tiger Adventures

Prepare
What do you know about species that are almost extinct? Have you ever seen a tiger in a zoo? Do you know how many tigers are left in the world and where they live? This activity will give you vital information about the tiger and other animals—fish, birds, and so on—that are in danger of disappearing from our world.

Perform
<http://www.5tigers.org/Directory/adventures.htm>
Go to the Web site listed above and select "Tiger on the Loose." In this adventure, you are the zoo director, and you learn that a rare tiger has escaped. Can you help the police find the tiger and return it safely to its home? Check out your skills. At this Web site, you can also track tiger poachers, build a good tiger home, and even pretend you are a Bengal tiger trying to survive. *Did you survive as a tiger or did you assist the police?*

Related Web Site

Risky Critters
<http://endangered.fws.gov/kids/risky.htm>
Some endangered species may not be around when your children or grandchildren grow up. Is this a concern for you? Do you think you know a lot about endangered animals? Take this quiz and see what you do know! When you finish, share the quiz and results with your family or with friends in your neighborhood. *How did you perform on the quiz?*

Connect Online: Web Learning Adventures

Name _____ Date _____

Exploration Activity
Subject Area: Social Studies

ACTIVITY 1 Country of Beauty—Belize

Prepare
Have you ever heard of Belize? Did you know that it is south of Mexico and lies between Guatemala and the Caribbean Sea? Although Belize is a small country, it has an enormous variety of things to see and do. Search for Belize on a map, and notice how close it is to the United States. This country, with the longest barrier reef in the Northern Hemisphere and over 60 percent of its land still covered by tropical forests, was once the center of the powerful Mayan civilization.

Perform
<http://www.travelbelize.org/guide/guidehp.html>
This tour presents four different perspectives on the small country of Belize. You can explore the country's rich Mayan history, wander through a sample of its protected areas of sea and land, or visit six unique districts and their major towns. Where do you want to begin? *What are some things you learned about Belize?*

Related Web Site
Belize EcoTourism
<http://www.belizeecotourism.org/>
Visit the Belize EcoTourism Center and learn about the ongoing struggle to protect the country's environment while encouraging tourism. Select one of the Projects/Plans and read about it. *Imagine you are an environmentalist. What do you think is the most pressing environmental issue facing Belize today? What solutions would you suggest to solve these problems?*

Connect Online: Web Learning Adventures

Name _____   Date _____

Exploration Activity
Subject Area: Science

ACTIVITY 2 Deserts—What Are They?

Prepare
What do you know about the deserts? Can you name any of the major deserts on Earth? Today the issues facing people in desert environments affect us all—from problems related to environmental protection, world food supplies, and agribusiness to questions about cultural diversity and biodiversity. As members of the global community, we must better understand desert regions.

Perform
<http://www.nasm.edu/ceps/drylands/>
Start your investigation of deserts with an overview of drylands and why they are important today. The site listed below tells what drylands are and then takes you on an excursion to learn why drylands are important, who the people are who live in the drylands, and the importance of water everywhere.

The following deserts are considered to be the largest and most significant in the world. From the site's homepage, select "What are Drylands?" and then click on the map at this site. Can you identify each desert on the map?

- **North American Deserts:** Great Basin, Mojave, Sonoran, Chihuahuan
- **South American Deserts:** Peruvian, Atacama, Patagonian
- **African Deserts:** Sahara, Negev, Namib, Kalahari
- **Middle East Deserts:** Jordanian, Arabian, Rub'al-Khali
- **Asian Deserts:** Kara Kum, Kyzyl Kum, Takla Makn, Gobi
- **Australian Deserts:** Great Sandy, Gibson, Great Victoria, Simpson

Related Web Site
Namib Desert
<http://www.greatestplaces.org/book_pages/namib2.htm>
This site provides an in-depth look at one of the most interesting deserts in the world. *What are some unusual features of the Namib Desert that you learned about at the site?*

Name _____ Date _____

Exploration Activity
Subject Area: Social Studies

ACTIVITY 3: A Person From History— Anne Frank

Prepare
Have you read the famous book *The Diary of Anne Frank*? It made a worldwide impact on teens and adults when it was first published after World War II. You may think that history is not very interesting or exciting, but when you read about events in history from the perspective of individuals your own age, you may change your mind.

Perform
<http://www.annefrank.com/site/af_life/1_life.htm>
At this site you will find an overview of Anne Frank's life and death, the words with which she detailed her years in hiding, and some information about others' experiences during that time. *Imagine that you are in a situation similar to Anne's—some circumstance that forces you to be in hiding somewhere. Then write a diary entry that briefly describes your situation and reflects your feelings, hopes, and fears about it.*

Related Web Site
Anne Frank House
<http://www.annefrank.nl/>
This site provides the opportunity to examine the rooms in which Anne Frank and her family hid for two years and also to look at other memorabilia connected with her and her family. You can also see the answers to questions that visitors to the site frequently ask. *What questions would you add to the site?*

Name _____ Date _____

Exploration Activity
Subject Area: Science

ACTIVITY 4 — Who's a Rube?

Prepare
Have you ever imagined a more interesting way to toast bread? Have you tried to imagine a machine that would make your bed? A man named Rube Goldberg created many cartoons showing just such machines, which depict the most elaborate and ridiculous devices to accomplish the most ordinary tasks. He became quite famous for them. This activity will help get your creative juices flowing, and perhaps you will think up a wacky (but workable) project yourself.

Perform
<http://www.rube-goldberg.com/>
Take a look at the official Rube Goldberg site. Read about his work and his Pulitzer Prize. Go to the Rube Goldberg Gallery at the site and select an "invention" to view one of his famous machines. You might find out that you have a knack for creating such machines, and soon you will wonder about the science and art involved in creating them. Notice also how inventive the names of the machines are. *In the spirit and style of Rube Goldberg, make up the names of five machines you would like to create. If you have time, you could even create a sketch of one of them.*

Related Web Site
Cabaret Mechanical Theatre
<http://www.cabaret.co.uk/>
Check out the marvelous coin-operated and push-button machines shown at this site. *Can you think of a mechanical device that you would like to make or create? Describe one such machine. Remember to give it a name.*

Connect Online: Web Learning Adventures

Name _____ Date _____

Exploration Activity
Subject Area: Science

Activity 5: Mars—the Red Planet

Prepare
Can you imagine living on Mars? Would you like to be one of the first human beings to do so? What would you need, and how can you learn more? First, think about what you know about Mars. Have you seen pictures or have you seen science fiction movies about this mysterious planet? Did you know that scientists are working to send astronauts there? Before you begin this activity, write down five things—sci-fi movies, people, random associations, or facts—that you associate with the planet Mars.

Perform
<http://mars.jpl.nasa.gov/>
Explore this site with its many resources about Mars. Learn about the explorations that are planned and the types of information that someone planning a trip to Mars would have to know. Look into the manned mission section, and also view the pictures that have been sent back from Mars. Go to the Kids' Corner, and read about the different activities you might consider doing. *What are some activities that you would like to try? Why do you think these activities would be good to do?*

Related Web Site

Kids Astronomy and Information about Mars
<http://www.kidsastronomy.com/mars.htm>
This site lets you explore a lot of information about Mars. Using the information you find at this site, try to answer the following questions:

1. How much would you weigh on Mars?
2. How far away is Mars from Earth?
3. What do you imagine the weather is like on Mars today?
4. What else would you like to know about Mars?

Connect Online: Web Learning Adventures

Name _____ Date _____

Exploration Activity
Subject Area: Health and Fitness

ACTIVITY 6 — Sports Alive!

Prepare

What sports do you like to play? Which sports are you involved with at school? Are there others that you play after school? Which ones do you like to follow on TV or in the newspaper? The World Wide Web is a great place to find out a lot about sports, how to play, and even where to buy the best equipment. What's more, it's a place to follow and learn about star players and to track the statistics about your favorite team.

Perform

<http://www.sikids.com/games/index.html>
<http://www.sikids.com/shorter/index.html>

Start this exploration at the *Sports Illustrated* site for kids. You will find interesting news about all sports, but there are also games and activities, stories of the athletes' lives, and much more. Choose a place of interest to begin and then roam around.

Then go to the Web site above and describe the life of one athlete you are interested in. *How did he or she become interested in sports? How much training did it take to become a successful athlete? What are some good examples you can learn from this person's life?*

Related Web Site

The National Baseball Hall of Fame and Museum
<http://baseballhalloffame.org/index.htm>

Check out the National Baseball Hall of Fame and Museum—is your favorite player in here? Select a favorite baseball team. This can be the team associated with the city where you live or another team you are interested in. Find out how long it has been since that team won the World Series. *What team has won the most World Series?*

Connect Online: Web Learning Adventures

Name _____ Date _____

Exploration Activity
Subject Area: Health and Fitness

Activity 7 — Pets To Love

Prepare
Do you have a pet now, or have you ever wanted to own a pet? Maybe you have thought about a different kind of pet. Maybe you have decided that when you have your own house you will get the pet you want. Do you think you have what it takes to be a good companion to an animal, to feed it and keep it healthy and clean? This exploration activity will provide you with information about a lot of pets, and perhaps it will clarify your idea of what kind of pet owner you would be.

Perform
<http://www.virtualdog.com/index_main_v4.html>
Since dogs are one of the most popular pets around, let's start with them. This site lets you choose a dog from dozens of types, read about that breed, and even name your new pet. You then take care of him or her, but you also have to use a limited amount of money carefully to keep your pet fed and healthy. Good luck! *Now that you are a pet owner, what are the things you will do for your dog daily, monthly, and yearly to keep him or her in good health?*

Related Web Site
The Animal Channel
<http://www.theanimalchannel.com/>
The Animal Channel has streaming video, articles about animals and pets in the news, and interactive activities. *What was the most interesting article you read?*

Connect Online: Web Learning Adventures

Name _____   Date _____

Exploration Activity
Subject Area: Economics

Activity 8 — Get a Job!

Prepare
Have you considered an after-school job? Perhaps you want to earn some extra money over the summer or begin saving for that car you have your eye on. You might want to think about the challenges of getting the job you want. This activity will give you the opportunity to learn about getting a job.

Perform
<http://www.sccis.org/main/main.htm>
This site provides all the information you need to start searching for the perfect after-school job. Use the information you find at the site to answer the following questions: *What are the responsibilities of the job you want? What skills do you need to get this job? How much do you think you'll earn if you work 10 hours a week?*

Related Web Site
ServeNet
<http://www.servenet.org/>
Perhaps you would rather give than receive. If you are not interested in working at a fast food restaurant, then try service learning. This is an opportunity to do something that earns more than money by helping agencies and local organizations. Explore the site. *What are some service learning jobs you would be interested in? What are some of the skills you would need to perform these jobs?*

Name _____ Date _____

Exploration Activity
Subject Area: Social Studies

Activity 9: The United Nations

Prepare
What do you know about the United Nations, also called the UN? Of course you have heard of it, but what does it do and how was it started? Would you ever be interested in visiting the UN or perhaps in working for it? Before you begin, consider what you already know about the UN.

Perform
<http://www.un.org/Pubs/CyberSchoolBus/untour/>
Take a historical look through pictures of the founding and development of the UN. Also take the visual tour of what the UN is doing right now and where it is concentrating its efforts. You can look at some of the remarkable art that is located in its New York City headquarters, such as the stained glass designed by Marc Chagall and the mosaic created by Norman Rockwell. *What are some things you learned about the United Nations? What would you like to know more about?*

Related Web Site
National Model UN
<http://www.nmun.org/>
Each year at this site students just like you create a model UN. Students assume the role of UN representatives. Each student studies a particular country. Then local, regional, and national UN meetings are held and significant issues are debated. Go to the site, and explore the current activities of the model UN. *What topics are currently being discussed?*

Connect Online: Web Learning Adventures

Name _____ Date _____

Exploration Activity
Subject Area: Computer Science

Activity 10 — Virtual Tours

Prepare
Have you heard of virtual reality? It can be defined as a computer program or application that allows for the creation of three-dimensional worlds. These virtual realities can be accessed from links on Web pages. They are displayed using a special VRML (virtual reality modeling language) viewer. This system can make you feel as if you are really viewing all aspects of a location, even though you are actually sitting at your computer.

Perform
<http://www.planet9.com/>
This site provides a wide range of exhibitions created using virtual reality. You can choose to see sports events or visit a planet. The choices change regularly, so you may want to visit often. *If you could design a virtual reality event, what would it be?*

Related Web Site
The Virtual Earth
<http://virtualearth.com/>
This site will take you around the world and allow you to visit many cities and locations. Select a city to visit and explore it. *What did you learn about this location, and what do you think about virtual reality in your future?*

Connect Online: Web Learning Adventures

Name _____ Date _____

Exploration Activity
Subject Area: Science

Activity 11 Keeping Watch

Prepare
How many zoos and aquariums have you visited? If you like to watch the animals but you get tired of standing around, then the animal cameras, also known as animal cams, may be a great way for you to keep watch. If there are special animals you are interested in observing but they live in zoos too far away for you to visit, animal cams may be your best bet for viewing them.

Perform
<http://natzoo.si.edu/Webcams/webcams.htm>
The Zoo TV site connected with the National Zoo in Washington, D.C., is the best place to watch live demonstrations of some of your favorite animals online. Check the best time to catch one of the live daily demos from the Elephant House. You can also tour the Naked Mole-Rat Burrow or tune in around the clock to see animals at their feeding times. After exploring the site, decide on your favorite demonstration. *What did you observe the animals doing?*

Use the Education Resources link to learn about the differences between African and Asian elephants. When you are ready, watch the Elephant Cam to see if you can pick out which elephant is which. *What are the characteristics that help you to distinguish one type of elephant from the other?*

Related Web Site
Panda Cam
<http://www.sandiegozoo.org/special/pandas/pandacam/index.html>
Everyone loves pandas, and the San Diego Zoo has one of the best cam sites for viewing them, including the mother panda and her cub. Watch the activities of Hua Mei, Bai Yun, and Shi Shi. *What did you observe about the interaction between baby pandas and their mothers? What are the similarities to the behavior of human babies and their mothers?*

Connect Online: Web Learning Adventures

Name _____ Date _____

Exploration Activity
Subject Area: Art and Music

Activity 12 Take Note

Prepare
What do you like to do—read about music, listen to it, or play it? In this activity, you'll do everything at Web sites that were created by students. You'll concentrate on learning to play the piano—online, of course. Then you will listen to audio clips and read interesting information about music.

Perform
<http://library.thinkquest.org/15060>
If you're looking for piano lessons, you're in luck. The ThinkQuest site listed below provides online lessons by using a virtual keyboard. Click the keys with your mouse, and tune in to how it sounds. The best place to start is to visit the "Lessons" section, where you'll find your personal Piano Tutor. You'll get an introduction to playing the piano, reading basic notes, and learning basic rhythm.

The fifteen lessons are targeted for beginning students, meaning those who have had no experience with music or the piano at all and who will advance to the beginning-intermediate level. If you already know how to play, you can brush up on your music theory and maybe even your sight-reading skills. Nearly all sections within this site invite you to add your own information, music files, graphics, or ideas. Other interactive features allow you to go to a virtual concert hall, organize your practice sessions, or play a variety of musical games.

Have you ever taken piano lessons before? How do these lessons compare? Do you think more people will learn instruments online in the future?

Related Web Site
Essentials of Music
<http://www.essentialsofmusic.com/main.html>
Learn about the major eras of classical music and the lives of classical composers. You can hear RealAudio clips of musical pieces and look up

definitions of musical terms in a glossary. Did you know that the composer Beethoven lost his hearing toward the end of his life? Read about this in his biography. *What symphonies did Beethoven write during the period when his hearing failed?*